THE CERTIFIED SALES PIONEER:

Proven lessons to become a great sales pioneer

By

Alaric Marrow

Table of contents

Introduction

The Certified sales Pioneer is composed in a simple to peruse conversational style. The book gives undertaking programming deals to pioneers and their agents ,demonstrated strategies to sell more by measuring business an incentive for the client and offering significant organization answers for C level leaders. No stunts, no alternate routes, basic manners by which deals pioneers can assist their agents with selling more programming by shutting more arrangements.

Practically month to month somebody asks me, "When are you going to compose a book". At the point when I inquire, "Why?", individuals tell me, "In light of the fact that nobody has composed a deals administration book with commonsense, answers for genuine issues in big business deals power",

Why:

62% of agents come up short, not on the grounds that they couldn't sell but since they were appointed some unacceptable records. Sales pioneers don't adjust ranges of abilities to account intricacy.

Agent wearing down all things considered SaaS organizations is more than 20%
Sales pioneers can't enroll A players

Sales Pioneers don't mentor their reps on bargain progression issues
Most deals pioneers are "celebrated scorekeepers"

Most sales pioneer don't rouse their outreach group
They're centered around bargains, not rep skill

Numerous salesforces just win half of their verification of ideas
They can't approach a triumphant POC Measures

8 of 10 leader purchasers say the deals gatherings they take are an exercise in futility.
Agents come up short on capacity to sell business esteem.

42% of reps in big business deals express one of the main 3 greatest difficulties is to lay out desperation. Reps don't evaluate basic business agony to make a purchasing impact.

Reps can't find significant level business champions, just low-level mentors
They can't track down torment over the commotion.

Numerous reps track down torment yet can't draw in a boss
They're childishly centered around bringing a deal to a close as opposed to procuring trust.

Most reps say they feel crazy during the deals interaction.
Reps can't find a hero to assist them with controlling the interaction.

half of reps say they can't beat cost complaints while organizations battle to build the typical arrangement size. Most agents are distributing, not selling.

Top sales pioneers will track down the responses to these issues and more in The Certified sales Pioneer

Chapter 1

THE QBR

For individuals who might be more up-to-date with business administration, QBR implies a quarterly business review. The QBR is an extraordinary discussion for project supervisors and venturesome salesmen to isolate themselves from the pack.
In any case, the worth of your QBR all really relies on how you direct it, what decisions you make, how profoundly you assess its plan, and how nicely you execute it.

1. Is it truly required?
Indeed and negative. Few out of every odd client is something similar. In this way, regardless of whether your client needs a QBR is dependent upon

the situation. Generally speaking, ensure you're taking a gander at it to increase the value of their business. Not as one more gathering with no genuine design or reason.

2. Would it be a good idea for it to be held quarterly or depending on the situation?
Another inquiry you should pose to yourself is at what recurrence would it be advisable for you to hold these business survey gatherings? Would it be a good idea for them to be held quarterly, month to month, or dependent upon the situation? It relies upon the intricacy of your client's business.

In the event that you are continually checking client use, you might track down different vulnerable sides. You shouldn't hang tight for a quarterly survey meeting to have these brought up.
You can require a gathering with a particular arrangement and show the way that they can accomplish additional worth from your item. This gathering can be planned for a more limited stretch dependent on the situation.
While, when the client's business results carve out an opportunity to reflect in their quarterly report, a

QBR can be valuable. This is essentially important in a complex B2B situation where business objectives are estimated and accomplished in months or years.

3. Would it be advisable for you to have Savvy or ambiguous objectives?
Understanding QBR's significance, you likely see that you should have an unmistakable objective ahead of time. Know the reason for a quarterly business survey, and you are bound to succeed. One of the most outstanding objective setting practices is having The Force of Brilliant Objectives. It discusses defining Brilliant objectives, which are:

Explicit
Your objective isn't simply "holding clients" yet a 90% degree of consistency, for instance.

Quantifiable
The objective isn't simply "to diminish the expense of obtaining" but to decrease it to 10% of the current expense toward 2022's last quarter's end.

Feasible
In the event that the beat rate is 30%, having an objective of lessening stir to 5% inside a quarter is unreasonable. A feasible objective should be to lessen it to 20% inside a quarter.

(This is only a model. Your setting characterizes the reachable objectives you can have).

Result-based
Result-based objectives make them genuine in execution. Process objectives, like leading a studio, are not outcome based. At the point when results can be estimated in view of the criticism of your activities, you can check in the event that your benchmarks are accomplished.

Time-bound
At long last, there ought to be a time span inside which you intend to accomplish your objective. In the event that no time period is given, you could carve out an opportunity to accomplish the objective. A particular period gets part of the responsibility for your arrangement for accomplishing objectives.

4. What ought to be the substance of a QBR? content of a QBR?
You need to go into this gathering ready, so being happy is significant.
All in all, what should your gathering contain?

Plan
Make a plan for the whole gathering and flow it to every one of the participants ahead of time through email.

Show Worth
During the last quarter, what business results have your clients accomplished through your item? Show esteem utilizing information.

Share Objectives
Subsequent to showing what they have accomplished, the best system is to show them what more they can accomplish from here on out. Share the objectives and benchmarks you plan for them to accomplish.

Share Your Activity Plan

Sharing objectives alone won't win a certainty, you'll likewise have to share your activity plan. An activity plan will assist with keeping everybody in total agreement on the subsequent stages and helps keep all gatherings responsible.

5. Would it be a good idea for you to gather client criticism in QBR?
Client criticism is a significant piece of QBRs. So, you shouldn't hold on until a QBR to check whether your clients are having issues in the event that you saw changes in their utilization. Notwithstanding, this criticism could assist you with resolving your clients' concerns with your item before the circumstance raises.

What are the different normal slip-ups that CCMs make while leading QBR?
Here is a portion of the normal slip-ups that CSMs make while leading QBR:

Straightforwardly bouncing into current realities
Each point you ought to cover in your QBR ought to prompt a conversation. While you could have a great deal that should be covered, your client could have a

ton to unload. However, you can't assist them with concentrating on the real issues at hand on the off chance that you're not having a functioning conversation with them.

No plan

Leading a QBR without a strong arrangement isn't useful to your clients. Regardless, they probably won't go to the following one on the off chance that they don't see the worth in it. Thus, make an arrangement for the gathering, clarify pressing issues, and guarantee the perfect individuals are joining in, so your client can get the greatest worth from it.

Focusing just on the past

While there ought to be some attention to past execution, the greater part of the gathering ought to zero in on future objectives.

Not considering sufficient support in the survey

Some CSMs inadvertently transform QBRS into speeches. Just covering the focus they possess and never passing on sufficient energy for their clients to share their contemplations. The best QBRs are a two-way discussion and technique meeting between you and your client.

No development
You can't accept your clients will remember all that was examined during your QBR. Regardless of whether they were locked in all through, individuals' neglect and miscommunication do occur. In this way, you ought to circle back to your clients after each gathering. Not in the least does this have a beneficial outcome on your clients, yet it'll assist all gatherings with getting a reasonable image of the focuses examined during the survey. It ought to permit clients to clear their questions and pose inquiries with a more open line of correspondence.

An excessive number of supervisors and reps consider QBRs straightforward record surveys, rather than a gathering where reps and deals with the board adjust area plans, and reps show their capacity to execute those plans.

Since us all in deals are objective situated, I'll give project leads a substantial objective: Your reps ought to think back on your QBRs, many quarters, and say, "Those were the hardest gatherings of my life, yet I sold more and procured more as a result of them."

Beneath I've framed three undeniable level inquiries each deal chief ought to pose to guarantee powerful QBRs for their reps and locale:

Question #1: What was the deal?
While last quarter's exhibition is still new, reps ought to convey a circumstances and logical results survey.
The arrangements we won last quarter and why
What we might have done any other way — and when — to pivot misfortunes
The arrangements we might have won, assuming we had been in the running
Project supervisors ought to zero in on profound thought and simple focus points during the QBR, not intricate introductions. Before you meet, convey the inquiries you anticipate that every rep should reply to. Try not to toss curveballs, particularly when different chiefs and leaders are in the room. You really want trust in their arrangement, and they need certainty that you have them covered.

Question #2: Could we at any point win?
Toward the finish of the quarter, reps can undoubtedly fail to focus on pipeline wellbeing. In light of this, the QBR is an ideal opportunity to survey your pipeline for:
Inclusion (pipeline isolated by share) for the impending quarter
The right blend of remote chances and okay arrangements
Bargains trapped in a particular phase of the deals cycle
Bargains guage out a few quarters that can be gotten
The necessities of possibilities who match your worth prop and channels
Realign with your reps on your ideal client profile. Try not to be shocked on the off chance that your most memorable QBRs with thorough pipeline examination result in a slimmer, and, surprisingly, more frightening, opportunity set. Forty genuine open doors are superior to 150 dart tosses.

Furthermore, don't hold on until the QBR examines the pipeline. In the initial two months of each and every quarter, make pipeline wellbeing part of your one-on-one discussions. Overcommunicate about how to offset close-term selling with pipeline building and know your base pipeline inclusion proportions. Be doubtful when a rep centers only around bargains far over your normal size, as they might seriously endanger the following two quarters.

Question #3: How might we win?
Each QBR ought to incorporate an estimate conversation and obligation to it. A supervisor should conclude whether his reps' arrangements convey certainty, in view of the accompanying:
The arrangements in their commit, best case, and most pessimistic scenario
For every one of those arrangements, the outcomes to date and the arrangement to close
At the point when a portion of those commit bargains definitely fail to work out, which arrangements will have their spot
Where the rep can find new arrangements that can be opened and shut in a similar quarter
These inquiries might feel scary, yet arrangement and action addressing must be based on a groundwork of trust — both a director's confidence in getting the straight story and a rep's confidence in the supervisor to help

What Are The Greatest
Advantages of QBRs?

At the point when done well, QBRs are gainful to both you and your clients. The following are a couple of advantages and major areas of strength:

Manufacture More grounded Connections

QBRs fortify organizations between your business and your clients.

Cut Further Chief Bonds

they cultivate connections between your leaders and your client's chiefs.

Flaunt return on initial capital investment

They allow you an opportunity to feature the return on the initial capital investment of your item and build up your worth to your client.

Make More clear Course

QBRs open up legitimate conversations about your clients' general well-being and how you might keep up with and work on that status.

Decrease Agreement Questions
QBRs assist with consoling you that your client will recharge their agreement or membership once it lapses.

Construct More Trust
They show to your client that you're significant about giving a return for capital invested and that you hope to do such within a 90-day time span.

Eventually, QBRs assist you with moving your client toward the path generally gainful to them — which normally will be the heading generally useful to you too. All things considered, on the off chance that the client doesn't encounter accomplishment with your item, there's a decent opportunity that client in the long run will stir — and that is not really great for one or the other party.

What To Remember for Your QBR
Over and over again, pioneers will regard QBRs as simply one more box to mark off the rundown, heading into gatherings with minimal vital vision. That is an expensive slip-up. QBRs are a significant opportunity to comprehend the worth your item at

present conveys to your clients, what they are searching for from now on, and help your organization's worth to key partners all through the association. Basically, the best QBRs follow a reasonable design and technique.

QBR Models and Tips to
Feed Your Organization's More extensive Objectives

Set up a QBR Plan
A QBR without a technique is a misuse of everybody's time. It additionally jeopardizes you of agitate. Make a plan and ensure all going to parties get it well in front of the gathering time. An engaged plan will set assumptions and make it more straightforward for clients to create their most significant inquiries or marks of conversation early.

Stress Business return on initial capital investment
QBRs are an opportunity to showcase return on initial capital investment and assist your clients with acknowledging esteem. That is the reason return for money invested ought to be a highlight of these gatherings. To figure out what return for capital

invested to zero in on, ask yourself, "For what reason did our client buy our item in any case, and over the last quarter, how well have we satisfied that need?" Present figures and information focus that exhibit the worth you have conveyed in that time span.

This is the ideal chance to return to the shared accomplishment designs that you created with your clients toward the start of the commitment. Keep tabs on your development, change timetables in light of new objectives or learnings your clients give, and consider what else is conceivable in view of the objectives you've proactively reached.

Keep the discussion customized to that particular client, the objectives they've illustrated, and what is workable for them in view of what you are familiar with their item reception and use. Invest the most energy during this piece of the QBR with the goal that you know precisely how to convey worth and assurance reestablishments, reception, and extension.

Present Benchmarking Information

Organizations love to perceive how well they're doing in contrast with their rivals. On the off chance that you can associate that accomplishment with your item utilizing hard measurements, they'll be anxious to keep working with you. Guarantee that you're taking note of what sticks out to your clients, what questions they ask, and what measurements they examine so your deals and advertising associations can utilize that data to drive extensions and upsells. While this may not be an ideal opportunity to make those upsells, it is critical to share the information learned with everyone and give any recognized significant bits of knowledge.

Set Up Your Next Quarterly Business Audit
Spread out significant objectives for the following quarter. Sometimes, this may be a great chance to raise extension valuable open doors or new items and additional items that will assist the organization with accomplishing its objectives. Make certain to affirm the objectives with your clients, frame who will be answerable for the different errands related to those objectives, and some other significant subtleties.

Keep in mind, that these gatherings should be vital and worth adding for your clients. At the same time, they should framework to your CSMs where the client needs to go, how to arrive, and any open doors later on that they ought to convey to the more extensive group.

Rest On Your Client Wellbeing File

Following the QBR, the CSMs ought to move immeasurably significant notes to that client's record and label exceedingly significant colleagues. The new setting will refresh their client's wellbeing score, which ought to likewise be shared among the bigger gathering. Give your most canny information as a client wellbeing list (CHI).

Utilizing a QBR Format

Now and then it's more straightforward to have a QBR format to follow as you're making gatherings.

At times, programming will try and give admittance to worked-in layouts that consolidate information that is being followed inside your occurrence. These prepared layouts make it simple to make redid, information-rich slides to direct your QBRs.

Nonetheless, in all cases, it's critical that you're conveying the information and not depending too vigorously on standard layouts. All things considered, one of the fundamental motivations to lead these gatherings, in any case, is to exhibit your extraordinary worth to the client as well as convey a feeling of how significant the client is to you. That implies each gathering — and the materials utilized at the gathering — ought to be custom-made explicitly to the client.

When drawn nearer insightfully, QBRs can assist with building spans between your organization and your clients, shaping solid associations that will endure all through the client lifecycle.

"... One of the imperative motivations to lead these gatherings, in any case, is to show your special worth to the client as well as convey a feeling of I show significant the client is to you."

Quarterly business surveys are a strong client achievement device, however, they simply scratch the surface with regards to driving undertaking wide client achievement. By zeroing in on a client-centered technique, it's feasible to transmit client accomplishment all through the whole association and impel the entire endeavor forward.

Chapter 2

THE DIRECTORS

A director is an individual who is liable for a piece of an organization, i.e., they 'make due to the organization. Supervisors might be responsible for a division and the individuals who work in it. Now and again, the director is responsible for the entire business. For instance, an 'eatery director is responsible for the entire café.

A director is an individual who practices administrative capabilities principally. They ought to have the ability to employ, fire, discipline, do execution examinations, and screen participation. They ought to likewise have the ability to endorse additional time and approve getaways. The individual is the chief.
The Chief's obligations likewise incorporate overseeing workers or a segment of the organization on an everyday premise.
Various kinds of supervisors

There is a wide range of sorts of supervisors across the entire range of an organization's or alternately element's progressive system.

Levels of The executives

Levels of executives spread from right at the highest point of an organization down to managers of little groups.

At the point when I utilize the word 'organization,' I'm additionally including 'association.'

Top Chiefs are responsible for an organization's technique. As such, they are the stewards of an association's vision and mission.

Useful Supervisors are liable for the viability and effectiveness of explicit regions of an organization, like showcasing. They are additionally responsible for faculty and records.

Group Directors or Administrative Chiefs are responsible for subgroups of a specific capability. They may likewise be responsible for a gathering of individuals from various pieces of the organization.

Line Chiefs are accountable for the result of specific items or administrations. They hold expertise in an

upward hierarchy of leadership, or over a specific product offering.
For instance, in a vehicle-production organization, the Line Chief may be responsible for the 'little vehicles' or 'light truck' division. Likewise, much more explicitly, they might be accountable for the 'little vehicles showcasing line.'

Head supervisors
Head supervisors are answerable for dealing with an income-delivering unit, for example, a product offering, a specialty unit, or a store.

The Senior supervisor needs to settle on choices across various capabilities inside that unit. Senior supervisors normally get a reward or commission when the unit gets along nicely.

Senior supervisors report to their top chiefs and take headings from them. The top leaders make sense of what the organization's general arrangement is. The Head supervisor thusly defines explicit objectives for the unit to find a place with the arrangement.

Senior administration alludes to the top supervisors of an organization, i.e., its chiefs. Assuming that I say, Harvard Business Audit is generally perused by senior administration, I mean organization chiefs.

Characteristics of a decent supervisor
Responsibility
Character
Social fondness
Prioritization
Warmth
Persistence
Genuineness
Definitiveness
Compassion
Uplifting outlook
Skill
Adaptability

Item Directors versus Brand Directors
Item Directors in for instance innovation organizations are normally the President of an item. They are likewise answerable for their technique, guide, and everything in regard to its creation.

Capacity and deals are additionally the Head supervisor's liability.
The position as a rule incorporates promoting, gauging, and benefit and misfortune obligations.
Brand Chiefs center around the insight and upkeep of a specific brand. They are not the same as Item Administrators.
The Brand Supervisor's occupation is frequently key, including significant level curation of both the association's picture and the reasonable moves toward keeping up with that picture.
The Brand Director expects to improve, keep up with, and support interest in the brand. There are areas of strength for on showcasing the organization's general picture. Brand chiefs rouse feeling, responses, and faithfulness.
Brand executives are normal in shopper item organizations. Item the executives, then again, is normal in programming firms.
This is on the grounds that customer item organizations need a top-of-the-mind review of their items and brands since they mass-market them.

As indicated by The board Study Guide:

"Brand the board is related with shopper item organizations through item the executives are related with programming organizations. This is on the grounds that customer item organizations need a top-of-the-brain review for their items and brands since they mass market them."

Derivation of administrator

The thing 'director' comes from the action word 'to make due,' which came to the UK around 1560. It came from Italian maneggiare 'to deal with' or 'to control a pony.' The Italian word came from the Latin thing manus 'hand.' The English word was likewise impacted by French manège 'horsemanship.'

The Web-based Derivation Word reference offers the accompanying remark in regards to the beginning of the English word 'supervisor': "1580s, 'one who makes due,' specialist thing from make due. The explicit feeling of 'one who leads a place of business or public foundation' is from 1705."

5 First concerns OF Exceptional Directors

Directors in the present associations influence both the business and its kin, both short and long haul. Our not set in stone what outstanding directors, need to do and how we make it happen, so our abilities in arranging, focusing on and it is fundamentally essential to contribute our time. The prior a chief bosses these abilities, the better prepared he is for this job, which today like never before previously, incorporates an overflow of strategic and vital requirements and potential chances to have an effect. We frequently move maneuvered away from our arranged exercises into putting out fires or last-minute gatherings, and our capacities to think rapidly, make changes and push ahead successfully expect that we apply an in general, undeniable level viewpoint on what's generally significant. This 10,000-foot view viewpoint is the foundation that keeps our needs front of mind and empowers us to acclimate to manage significant, spontaneous occasions without losing center.

As far as I can tell as a specialist, I have worked with leaders, ranking directors, center chiefs, and managers in different enterprises - machine shops, plastics, hardware, synthetic, printing, designing and assembling, inside associations both little and enormous. I've found that really remarkable directors share the 5 first concerns for all intents and purposes. While these chiefs ordinarily zig and zoom to manage pressing circumstances and impromptu authoritative requirements, they guarantee they set aside a few minutes for successful work on these 5 fundamentals. On occasion, they might invest less energy than arranged, yet every one of the 5 first concerns is a ball that isn't dropped. Their 10,000-foot view point of view fills the significant need of keeping the best 5 needs front-of-mind, driving their prosperity, that of their immediate reports, and of others in their range of impact.

The best 5 needs are:

1. Connections: In the event that you take a gander at your own range of impact, you can recognize the people who influence you most, and who you influence. You influence these individuals in numerous ways, like by your presence or nonappearance, your activities, words, choices, and

business-related transforms you make. Instances of individuals in [what I call] your range of impact incorporate associates, peers, our prompt chiefs, inner clients, and individuals who report to you. (An individual's range of impact likewise incorporates individuals near her external work, yet to keep this article brief we'll zero in on work connections.) The best directors put a high need on treating individuals well and on keeping up areas of strength for viable work associations with the vital individuals in our range of impact. We make time to get to know them, connect with them, address their issues, help them, remember them for a dynamic that influences them, request their feedback and criticism, and start positive cooperation with them.

Business Procedure Execution: Supervisors own liability regarding zeroing in their associations on accomplishing vital objectives. Of specific significance is following through on the organization's incentive or separation. Zeroing in on the business procedure empowers individuals to focus on actually, and pursue different occupation-related choices. The system likewise gives a setting to change. Pioneers who assist their kin with making the association between their jobs and the system, and between authoritative changes and the methodology, fabricate worker responsibility and commitment. Note: The 5 keys to system execution displayed in the infographic on the right will be the subject of one more post in June. They incorporate structure and essential comprehension among your kin, accomplishing the most extreme advantage from adjusted measurements, building initiative believability, adjusting work exercises, association design and culture with the business technique, drawing in, creating, and holding ability. Remembered for every one of the 5 is market discipline, which is the capacity to conclude the incentive/separation for the business.

3. Nonstop Getting the hang of Remarkable supervisors to keep awake to date with abilities and industry advancements through systems administration, ordinary, continuous perusing, and occasionally going to chosen meetings and instructive occasions. They share articles with their kin and talk about them in group gatherings or one-on-ones. They urge their kin to do likewise. They put resources into fostering their kin in regions that

empower them to follow through on the association's technique, as well as to guarantee individuals have the information and abilities expected to meet the association's future requirements. They have group conversations expecting and addressing snags to association execution, and they encourage gaining from both astounding and disheartening execution results. They energize facilitated trial and error for advancement and improvement through experimental runs programs inside and across capabilities.

4. Toolbox: "Be ready" isn't just a scout proverb. It's likewise one of the standards the best administrators live by. For this situation, it's tied in with having devices and assets helpful to the pioneer. Models incorporate things that upgrade one's capacity to impart successfully to people and gatherings about the business methodology and measurements, explicit encounters and stories to share, articles, books, DVDs, flip-diagrams, and markers for conceptualizing, and they apply perceived viable critical thinking and dynamic strategies. The toolbox of an exceptional pioneer likewise incorporates

preparing materials from past advancement programs on initiative and the board and other business or industry-related subjects, for reference as well with respect to instructing and creating individuals. The tool compartment additionally incorporates tests of items and parts, things illustrative of the organization's set of experiences, client letters, grants the organization has won, and distributions by pioneers in the business.

5. Wellbeing: You might be shocked to hear that the greater part of the exceptional pioneers I've realized set aside a few minutes for practice consistently, previously or after work, or during lunch.

They additionally have standard meetings with specialists and dental specialists. The best chiefs focus on their well-being, remembering it assists them with managing pressure and playing out their best over the long haul. They likewise give adaptability to empower their kin to deal with their wellbeing.

Chapter 3

The B2B SALES PROCESS

A B2B deals process is a bunch of steps intended to assist salesmen with changing over possibilities into clients. It's a versatile, repeatable guidance manual for deals achievement.

In this book, we will go through our deals cycle bit by bit and investigate why having one is so essential for a scaling organization.

Why you ought to foster a B2B deals process
Most salesmen partake in the opportunity that accompanies their job. The capacity to acquire their character to each cold pitch and adjust to evolving discussions. Be that as it may, the best salesmen aren't craftsmen, they're researchers. They use B2B information to frame bits of knowledge and make major areas of strength for a cycle.

A deals cycle gives a system whereupon a salesman can make do while giving four extra advantages:

Having a more unbending cycle setup makes it simpler for new starters to get cutting-edge.
Breaking a deal system into stages makes it simpler to recognize perspectives that aren't working, and change them.
Having an additional organized deals approach will make it difficult to disregard significant stages.
Seeing where clients are in the deals cycle makes it simpler to gauge all the more precisely.
The B2B deals process made sense of
The primary thing to do before you begin prospecting is to investigate your objective market and characterize the Absolute Addressable Market (or Cap). Whenever you've done this, you will be prepared to launch the deals interaction.

I've broken our one into 8 separate stages, which are illustrated in the infographic beneath. This is a B2B deals process!

The 8 phases of each and every B2B deals process

1 - Lead age
Lead age is the most common way of tracking down qualified leads; individuals who've communicated

interest in your item and who you ought to connect with! In the event that you have a decent comprehension of your complete addressable market and the right lead age programming setup, this step ought to require some investment by any means!
!

2 - Disclosure
Each great sales rep ought to know pretty much everything there is to know about their item. Each incredible salesman ought to likewise grasp their possibility's business. By placing in the basis and attempting to comprehend the possibility's problem areas before you talk with them, you'll have the option to furnish them with arrangements. This examination stage sets you up for deals disclosure calls.

Investigating the possibility likewise offers you a chance to qualify the lead before you get the telephone. Here are a few hints:

Associate with the possibility on LinkedIn. Actually, take a look at their new movement. What have they remarked on? What have they shared? Have they

composed any articles or been highlighted in another person? Experiences like these can be perfect for building compatibility on your cold pitches.
Click on their organization's site. Have they distributed any reports or official statements as of late? Look at their blog, assuming they have one. Observe the language/terms that are utilized by the organization. Once more, this is all great data that you can use in your calls.
Find out about the most recent news in their area. Buy into industry news sites or LinkedIn gatherings. At the point when you call the possibility, you need to seem like a specialist - in your field, yet at the same in theirs!
The primary concern is - despite the fact that disclosure can require some investment, it'll settle your decisions undeniably more effectively.

3 - Capability
Now that you've done the foundation, now is the right time to get on the telephone.

During the main segment of your deals call, you ought to utilize a lead scoring framework to evaluate the possibility's reasonableness as a client.

Ask them unassuming inquiries, toss in some key-business phrasing, center around their concerns and decide if you could tackle them. If not - don't compel it!

There's no time to waste, and in the event that you have a decent lead list, you'll have a lot of others to address!

4 - Pitch

You ought to by this point have a smart thought of the battles the possibility faces. Provided that this is true, you'll have the option to convey a pitch that is customized to tackle their concerns.

This is where your imagination comes in. The most point-by-point deals process on the planet can't supplant Moxy or charm...this is the reason we frequently stay away from nitty-gritty contents.

A decent prearranged attempt to close the deal should go on for something like 30 seconds. During this time, you'll have to show the possibility that you've done all the necessary investigation. Hit on central issues of significant worth which are applicable to them. Here are a few hints:

Quote the kinds of organizations that the possibility's organization possibilities to - this is an extraordinary method for exhibiting that you've done all necessary investigation!
Excite interest in the possibility. Try not to over-make sense of your item or administration; you maintain that the possibility should circle back to certain inquiries.
An attempt to seal the deal isn't a reason to list your great elements in general. Possibilities would rather not hear it! Center rather around how your item can help them. What results might they at any point hope to check whether they turn into a client?

5 - Complaint taking care of
A possibility will seldom be prepared to purchase following your pitch. They'll in all probability have inquiries which you'll have to reply to.
With regards to protest taking care of, the possibility is rarely off-base. On the off chance that you absolutely can't help contradicting a possibility's complaint, they'll hang up. All things being equal, pay attention to what they need to say, and reposition your proposal in a way that responds to

their inquiry. The odds are good that they've recently not heard the right data yet.
Over the long run, you'll foster a munitions stockpile of protest goals. Up to that point, simply stand by listening to the deal's complaint, recognize it, and propose a sensible arrangement. Assuming that this works out in a good way, it'll be an ideal opportunity to settle the negotiation.

6 - Shutting
This phase of the B2B deals interaction ought to be the most thrilling part of the possibility. You've exhibited the worth of your item, taken care of all of their cold pitch complaints, and persuaded the possibility that your answer is a venture that can't be missed!

Examine costs and arrange if fundamental. Offering a free increased value of the arrangement can assist with getting it over the line.
Additionally, make certain to examine each of the excess strides before the call closes, including talking to pretty much every one of the partners that need to approve the arrangement. This will guarantee that there are no astonishing knocks en

route; presently the marked agreement will be in sight!

7 - Follow up
After the deals call, send the possibility a subsequent email. Because of the number of individuals that are normally engaged with marking a B2B buy, you must have a decent impression!
Keep it proficient and give the following stages. Incorporate a rundown or (surprisingly better!) a recording of your discussion, as well as any extra valuable data. Leaving the discussion optimistically will invite rehash sales and upsells.
Furthermore, in the event that you will keep working with the new client, you'll start your new working relationship off in great shape.
Top tip: an effective method for being proficient is through a deals email signature.

8 - Check-in
Congrats! Your objective possibility has turned into the client. There's only one stage left.
After you've trusted that the client will see the worth of your item, it merits contacting them one final

time. Check-in with them to perceive how they're doing.

Chapter 4

DISSECTING BARGAIN MOVEMENT

The outreach group is perhaps of the most datum-driven divisions in an association where most parts of the deals cycle are quantifiable. Measurements that educate deals experts concerning the strength of deals procedures and income age are significant for examining the presentation and adequacy of strategic policies. Accordingly, it's vital to gather and investigate deals information for independent direction and methodology advancement. In this article, we examine what deal examination is, the reason for estimating deals execution, how to break down deals execution and what measurements should consider.

What is a deals investigation?

Deals investigation is the most common way of gathering, assessing, and applying information about different deals processes. For example, deals information can perceive organizations about marketing projections, income values, client maintenance, and obtaining rates and general benefit. SA deals investigation is a powerful instrument that directors can use as indicated by a few strategies, all determined to give a more extensive viewpoint of deals exercises. You can follow deals execution measurements, break down them and distinguish parts of your association's practices that help deals and deals processes that need improvement.

For what reason is it vital to dissect your deal's execution?
Other than acquiring significant knowledge into by and large benefit and market position, dissecting deals execution can help your association:

Further, develop client support
Different deal measurements can assist you with a better comprehension of client needs. For instance, an expansion in conveyance orders can assist you with distinguishing the ways to deal with taking to guarantee persistent admittance to your organization's items and economical techniques for circulating items to clients. Deals investigation can likewise assist you with understanding elective

items your clients buy that help the utilization or use of your association's items. Understanding this information can help outreach groups strategically pitch comparable items, suggest elective items, and better help consumer loyalty.

Distinguish beneficial client markets

Examining deals execution can likewise assist your organization with characterizing objective business sectors, fostering designs for arriving at possible clients, and laying out associations with target clients. During an examination of target markets, outreach groups can then recognize qualities and client personas and fragment markets to more readily target publicizing and special materials. You can likewise profit from deals examination since understanding what sections are the most beneficial for your organization can assist you with making extra strategies for arriving at comparative business sectors to help future development.

Support group choices

Deals investigation gives colossal execution information on the advancement of your deals plan, execution of deals procedures, and execution of colleagues. You can utilize the different measurements of deals investigation to settle on conclusions about these different parts of deals, for example, which techniques to execute, how to prepare agents, what ways to deal with taking while examining chance, and how to draw in with client markets. Chiefs can impart significant objectives to senior and mid-supervisory group individuals, who can then immediately lead deals, advertising, and client service groups in further developing cycles and meeting business objectives.

Step-by-step instructions to investigate deals execution

Utilize the accompanying moves toward breaking down deals execution so you and your group can foster effective techniques to build income and consumer loyalty:

1. Recognize the business information to dissect

It's essential to initially figure out what deals information you need to dissect and use for system improvement and further developing execution. For example, consider information like consumer loyalty rates, top-selling items, and buying propensities for rehash clients. This data can then assist you to impart patterns in deals exercises with key partners so your organization can lay out compelling objectives for expanding income and development.

2. Team up with partners
It's fundamental to team up with different deals partners subsequent to recognizing key deals execution measurements and breaking down information. During the coordinated effort process, group layout deals with targets and benefit objectives, which can help outreach groups decide the best methodologies for supporting the accomplishment of fruitful results. When you and your groups team up with the board and partners, you can utilize the information to quantify deals action, make gauges, and plan for enhancements.

3. Make and present a marketing chart
Eventually, a deals execution investigation can be a fundamental instrument for creating exact deals figures. Utilizing the information you acquired from accumulating, examining, and teaming up with partners, your group can arrange significant information that provides chiefs with a thought of

what you hope to achieve from here on out. A few components of your deals execution examination that can prompt more exact estimates to incorporate normal deals income per bookkeeping period, normal client procurement per period, normal creation costs, normal promoting and publicizing spend per period, and in general benefit from deals.

Consider the accompanying 10 deals measurements to help the course of your deals investigation:

1. Deals development
Deals development is one more term for income development and it looks at the ongoing income to the past income. It is typically one of the fundamental presentation pointers since it straightforwardly influences the net revenue. A deals investigation generally gauges deals development over a predefined period, for example, each month, quarter per year, contingent upon the association. The key presentation markers in deals development are positive and negative development inside the predetermined time, where positive development shows achievement and productivity and negative development shows a reduction in benefit.

2. Deals Target
The deals target is a worth that project supervisors use to look at current and future deals incomes. For example, deal targets can be the number of units sold or the number of client accounts a business gets. Checking deals targets can guarantee groups comprehend how really they're outperforming past shares and can uphold improvement plans for helping efficiency.

3. Deals to date
The deals to date metric is an assessment of deals exchanges that happen within a predetermined period. Organizations use deals to date to contrast past numbers and current marketing projections to comprehend how execution changes over the long run. Team leads frequently contrast deals with dates utilizing yearly periods. One of the most fundamental key exhibition markers inside the deals to date is the increment or decline of deals inside the period you measure.

4. Item execution

The item execution metric is great for organizations with different items. Item execution breaks down the deals of every item to assist organizations with figuring out which items have the best exhibition. This measurement can likewise assist you with distinguishing lower-performing items so you can recognize the qualities that need improvement or change.

5. Cannibalization rate
Cannibalization rate estimates what the productivity of option or swap items means for the benefit of more seasoned items. This measurement gives an understanding of how much benefit misfortune you can expect because of another item sent off, giving groups data to foster procedures that help the proceed with the progress of the first item. Along these lines, understanding how clients view recently acquainted items in examination with unique or obsolete items can assist your organization with recognizing ways to deal with refreshing, improving, or reestablishing unique item forms.

6. Lead change rate

The lead change rate estimates the rate at which your outreach group changes over possible clients into paying clients. You can decide your lead change rate by isolating the number of leads you get through promoting exercises by the number of leads that make a buy. This measurement can give knowledge into how successful your advertising strategies are at contacting applicable crowds, making a commitment, and propelling buys.

7. Sell-through rate

The sell-through rate is another significant deals execution metric that can give you an understanding of the stock your organization sells in something like a month that it gets from producers, merchants, or providers. It's likewise a significant measurement for checking inventory network proficiency and can uphold finance groups while making deal figures.

8. Deals by district

Deals by the district are a significant measurement for organizations that perform whole business processes across various areas. For example, a provincial organization might perform deals exercises all through every one of the country's states. For this situation, the provincial company can quantify the exhibition of its different areas to comprehend where its items are of the most interest. This measurement likewise assists organizations with knowing which items are most productive and cutthroat on the lookout.

9. Deals per delegate

Outreach groups are fundamental in drawing in clients and keeping up with client connections, bringing about effective deals exchanges, rehashing business, and expansions in income. It's significant, in this way, to guarantee outreach groups have sufficient preparation to foster the abilities and methods important to help and further develop the client experience. At the point when agents have the apparatuses and assets they need to succeed, they're bound to have better execution, marketing projections, and consumer loyalty rates.

Chapter 5

ANTICIPATING SYSTEM

Key gauging assists with powerful preparation. Organizations use techniques to arrive at their objectives. One of the critical components of an organization's tasks is estimating what objectives are sensible, and how much the organization will accomplish them. Key determining joins the two capabilities, changing conjectures to help vital objectives, and utilizing working techniques to guarantee that these figures are exact. Private companies once in a while make gauges and over and over miss their objectives. Incorporating gauging into their business techniques can build the exactness of their gauges and assist them with arriving at the objectives they set.

Systems

An essential way to deal with business tasks sets targets matching the organization's drawn-out objectives and distinguishes drives that will permit the organization to contact them. The organization carries out the methodologies and checks whether the outcomes are in accordance with the objectives. In the event that not, the organization needs to change procedures and execute new drives. Run-of-the-mill key instruments are financial plans and timetables. A common drive might determine that the organization needs to arrive at a particular deal volume for a specific item by a specific date.

Anticipating

Organizations not took part in essential gauging treat estimating as a different capability. Organizations attempt to gauge the way of behaving of the factors of their business climate and show up at potential deals and benefit figures. They base their methodologies on sensible targets drawn from these figures. Numerous private ventures utilize this straightforward approach and when they miss their objectives they fault surprising varieties in the business climate for mistaken figures and attempt to improve during the following cycle.

Climate

Vital determining unites the two capabilities by setting the gauges in a particular climate. Organization systems incorporate impacting the climate to relate to that utilized for gauges. Simultaneously, organizations perceive that changing factors in the climate might impact figures. Organizations incorporate the figures powerfully in the essential targets so that in the event that the climate and the conjectures change, the objectives can change too. Along these lines, organizations utilize their working climate to decisively connect the gauging and arranging capabilities, working on the exhibition of both.

Choices

At the point when organizations utilize vital estimating along these lines, it allows them to pursue choices that all the more precisely mirror what is happening. In the event that a specific expense variable goes up startlingly, the organization can see the impact on the figures and targets. It can respond by making up for the expense change or by changing focuses to reflect it. Key determining makes the organization's tasks delicate to showcase factors consistently. Organizations can choose whether to appoint extra assets for a restorative activity or to change their methodologies to mirror what is happening.

What is Gauging?
Anticipating alludes to the act of foreseeing what will occur later on by thinking about occasions at various times. Essentially, it is a dynamic instrument that assists organizations with adapting to the effect of representing things to come to a vulnerability by inspecting verifiable information and patterns. It is an arranging device that empowers organizations to diagram their best courses of action and make financial plans that will ideally cover anything vulnerabilities might happen.

Planning versus Estimating
One thing that is certainly obvious is that planning and gauging are the two devices that assist organizations with anticipating their future. Be that as it may, the two are unmistakably divergent in numerous ways. We should think about the accompanying focuses:

Planning includes making an explanation that comprises various monetary exercises of an organization for a particular period, for example, projected income, costs, income, and ventures. It is normally not led exclusively by one division, say, the money office, since it requires input from different offices to concoct an all-encompassing and point-by-point report. In this way, the planning system carves out the opportunity to finish. The organization utilizes the spending plan to direct it in its monetary exercises.

While spending plans are normally made for a whole year, figures are typically refreshed month to month or quarterly. Through gauging, an organization can change its spending plan and dispense more assets to a division, depending on the situation, it is predicted to rely on what. In rundown, spending plans rely upon the gauge.

Gauging Techniques

Organizations pick between two fundamental techniques when they need to foresee what might potentially occur from here on out, specifically, subjective and quantitative strategies.

1. Subjective technique

Also called the critical strategy, subjective anticipating offers abstract outcomes, as it is involved individual decisions by specialists or forecasters. Gauges are frequently one-sided in light of the fact that they depend on the master's information, instinct, and experience, and seldom on information, making the cycle non-numerical.

One model is the point at which an individual figures the result of a finals game in the NBA, which, obviously, depends more on private inspiration and interest. The shortcoming of such a strategy is that it tends to be mistaken.

2. Quantitative strategy

The quantitative strategy for estimating is a numerical interaction, making it predictable and objective. It guides from putting together the outcomes with respect to assessment and instinct, rather than using a lot of information and figures that are deciphered.

Elements of Gauging

Here is a portion of the elements of making a gauge:

1. Includes future occasions

Figures are made to anticipate the future, making them significant for arranging.

2. In view of over a wide span of time occasions
Gauges depend on feelings, instinct, and surmises, as well as on realities, figures, and other significant information. Each of the elements that go into making an estimate reflects somewhat what occurred with the business previously and what is thought of as prone to happen from here on out.

3. Utilizes anticipating procedures
Most organizations utilize the quantitative strategy, especially in arranging and planning.

The Most common way of Estimating
Forecasters need to follow a cautious cycle to yield exact outcomes. Here are a few stages all the while:

1. Foster the premise of determining
The most important phase in the process is fostering the premise of the examination of the organization's condition and recognizing where the business is as of now situated on the lookout.
2. Gauge the future tasks of the business
In view of the examination led during the initial step, the second piece of gauging includes assessing what's in store states of the business where the

business works and anticipating and breaking down how the organization will admission.

3. Control the conjecture

This includes taking a gander at various gauges previously and contrasting them and the genuine things that occurred with the business. The distinctions in past outcomes and current estimates are dissected, and the explanations behind the deviations are thought of.

4. Audit the cycle

Each step is checked, and refinements and changes are made.

Wellsprings of Information for Gauging

1. Essential sources

Data from essential sources get some margin to accumulate on the grounds that it is direct data, likewise viewed as the most dependable and reliable kind of data. The forecaster himself does the assortment and may do such through things like meetings, surveys, and center gatherings.

2. Optional sources

Optional sources supply data that has been gathered and distributed by different elements. An illustration of this sort of data may be industry reports. As this data has previously been gathered and dissected, it makes the interaction speed.

Conclusion

This book is a significant wellspring of data for B2B salesmen, supervisors, pioneers and groups. It shares lessons of changing a low performing outreach group into an incredible, viable selling motor, giving bit by bit of knowledge on the what, how and why en route.

www.ingramcontent.com/pod-product-compliance
Lightning Source LLC
LaVergne TN
LVHW050343160826
845677LV00014B/3759